All the Things I See

JENNY JOSEPH

All the Things I See

Selected Poems for Children

MACMILLAN
CHILDREN'S BOOKS

First published 2000 by Macmillan Children's Books

This edition published 2001 by Macmillan Children's Books
a division of Macmillan Publishers Ltd
20 New Wharf Road, London N1 9RR
Basingstoke and Oxford
www.panmacmillan.com

Associated companies throughout the world

ISBN 0 330 39150 X

3 5 7 9 8 6 4 2

A CIP catalogue record for this book is available from the British Library.

Printed by Mackays of Chatham plc, Chatham, Kent

Contents

Singing

Of speckled eggs the birdie sings
 And nests among the trees;
The sailor sings of ropes and things
 In ships upon the seas.

The children sing in far Japan,
 The children sing in Spain;
The organ with the organ man
 Is singing in the rain.

Robert Louis Stevenson

Dance for your Daddy
My little laddy
Dance for your Daddy
My little man.

You shall have a fishy
In a silver dishy
You shall have a fishy
When the boats come home.

Anon.

*This book is dedicated to the children
who dance and sing*

The things I see

Hurry hurry hurry
It won't do you no good though.
The lights ahead are red
You go up to them slap bang
Rocking on your chassis.
Meanwhile you have missed
What I have seen –
A small boy hiding behind a tree
And the buds breaking out all around him, kissed
With little tongues of green.

Angry angry angry
It won't do you no good though.
For the catch on the door will slide
When you push your boxes through at that hasty angle.
The red fuming skin of your face
Must be all your eyes can see.
Meanwhile you have missed
What I have seen –
A woman with a strange patched face
Looking up into the spring sky through the mist
In her light eyes, for Heaven's Queen.

Furry furry furry
It won't do you much good though
To be wrapped so warm to the eyes
That you cannot turn your head
That you miss what I have seen –
All the things I see:
A tall man like a pole
And at the bottom of his long arms, down at his feet

A tiny little pushchair and a tiny baby
Sunk in its hammocky seat between the wheels;
A little girl sitting high up on her father's arm
With a long furry tail laid heavy among her ringlets
Swinging from her Davy Crockett hat;
And two extraordinary pigeons
Of quite different and glistening colours.
And a cloak of St Francis brown and a Mary's blue
Walking together collecting the dust of the street
All the things that I see
As I hurry hurry hurry
To work, but slowly, slowly.

Coming up our street

Everything is news to me
The grit on the pavement winks with a new eye.
The angle of the building never signals the same way twice
As I turn round it home.

What face will be looking out of the picture this time?
What voices call when I open the twice-read book?
The future is tucked in corners with the past
The air is loaded with things we have not in mind.
So I turn round the corner, the last before I get home
For there is the house appearing much as I left it
Its outline still real against my bit of the sky.

Getting back home

Hang your hat on the peg
Rest up, rest up
Fling your coat on the bed
For you have travelled many miles to see me.

Put your feet on the bench
Rest up, rest up
Heave off your heavy boots
For you have come through winter days to see me.

Settle down by the fire
Rest up, rest up
Lean back and smile at me
For after all this time and travelling
Oh traveller, I'm glad to see you.

The un-developers

The little cats sit under the hedge
The many small offspring of a great big tabby
Who lives out of sight round the other side of the house
They are watching the pigeons in the road.
The pigeons strut and flirt and think no danger.
Children are delighted with the cats
And cajole them as they are tugged along by Mum;
An old woman puts down crumbs for the birds
And cars pass in between.
The cats purr and the pigeons peck up the fodder
But they are waiting for interruptions of humans to pass
So they can get on with what they are doing:
Five little kittens lurking and stalking big birds
And foolish pigeons flirt-flirting in the road.

Going out with you

Cherry red lips
And a cherry red nose,
Eyes like brown berries
And tappety toes

In polished brown shoes
That gleam like your eyes
That follow the quick bird
That calls as it flies,

O cherry red lovely
My gorgeous fruit pie
Who could be happier
Than you, sweet, and I?

Poem for a country child

There was a bird and he went hop hop
There was a bird that sang so sweet
It wasn't a robin, a cock or a linnet
It wasn't a cuckoo, a crow or a pigeon
But my own sweet bird.

There was a cow and she went plod plod
There was a cow and she breathed so warm
She wasn't a Friesian, a brindle, a Shorthorn
She wasn't a Jersey, piebald, a fierce one
But my own dear cow.

There was a garden and it was mine.
It wasn't a show place, there wasn't a lawn.
There was an old swing and a broken-down fence
And a pile for a bonfire and birds that came hop
Hop hop to my feet if I sat very still
And cows that moved slowly in the green field
My sweet green field.

Poem for a town child

My Dad took me to look in a shop window
Because it was going to be my birthday.
In it there was everything round:
There was a round pot made of a thin strippy snake
Like the ones we did at school, only better.
There was a round mat made of round thin rope
Like the one my sister brought home that I thought was good
Only the shop one was not so hairy.
There was a round glass ball on a stand with things inside
That seemed to change when you moved your head down
    to look
And I wanted that more than anything
Only my Dad said it was very expensive.
But the best of all was the roundest thing there
It was a snail and it was round all the way round
And whenever you started to go round it you had to go on
    to the top
And then back round again you couldn't stop
Till your eye reached where you began. It was like a puzzle
And much better done than the coily pots and the twisty
    mats, though they were good,
But my Dad said it was part of the decoration, not for sale
And anyway he wanted to buy me a present, not an old snail
That you could find any time in the yard

But that was the best thing there and that was what I wanted
And I thought if we went in and I said that to the man
He might give me one
But my Dad didn't want to.

Makers

Of my chair

Three wicker wands
Made with hands
That think nothing, but know
That this is how they're meant to go
Not for any reason
Except that it is so.
It is the chair he's good at making, not the thought.

Of my candlestick

Here was a calm man
Knew how to put three curves together.
If I could bend a piece of metal so
As to coil the arc my fingers bent, round hearts
There would be nothing in words I'd need to do or know.

Cover up

A trowel-depth under soil's surface –
The colour of rotting leaf or dog muck
I stirred a fat healthy toad.
Cover him up, cover him up
Don't disturb his spring-time.

Lying with the grubs, a thick white shoot.
Cover it up, cover it up
Don't disturb its spring-time.

Looking in a drawer
Riffling through the scarves and socks
My fingers met a hard box.
Cover it up, cover it up
Don't disturb the surprise,
Don't undo the secret.

And, Grown-ups,
Coming across the growing children's games
Do not ask or pry
Do not dig or order
Or try to understand.
Cover up what you know
Let be, let them be.

Impressions of travel

1. Balconies of Italy   Oleander, Rosemary
    Hillside of Italy   baked beige houses, vigneroles
    Children of Italy   silk-skinned, beautiful, mortal.

2. 'Private keep out'. (Notice on foreshore.)

Who can own the sea?
I can, I can, say the Americas.

The hulk in the bay
And the gulls' cry with the ocean's voice in it,
Harsh and mournful echo free on the wind

Say otherwise.

3. Leaving Maine. 'Thank you for having me'

I would've sent flowers
The day so sparkling and my heart so light
Soaring but steady   like the geese flying
Their wings' thrum thrum carrying them to Canada.

Flowers –
Or, stopped at a jeweller's, diamonds to hang from your ears
As the fuchsia drips its pendicles from dark leaves.

Flowers, though, you have in your child's blooming,
Her skin the silk of petals,
And diamonds you have when the sun, sailing through fog
Steadies the drops that the spruce holds in the far quiet forest.

4. The traveller

On the left hand the moon
On the right hand my friends
Frosty roads lead ahead
Straight eye, light hand, firm heart.

5. Moon and flowers

If there were flowers on the moon,
And sharp and bright and eerie that would be,
They would be like the Laws of Nature,
Like the light from the stars.

But our flowers are rooted in colour
And they are mortal.

Humans and animals

It would be nice to be a bird
And not mind the wet;
Not to have to scrunch up,
Not to have to be brave getting into the river:
Holding our breath, screwing up our eyes, flinching into a jelly,
But to continue with our purposes like the horse
Who grazes at the same pace in an open field
When arrows of rain fall thick, silvering
The pall which obscures the meadow as it comes down.

The imminent desertion

O birds gathering in the skies
What takes you on your long journeys?

Can our desire not keep you here
But you must scatter through the air
That has for months been blue and clear.
Can nothing keep you anywhere?

O birds preparing for the skies
What takes you on your long journeys?

Will you not stay and keep the sun,
On its desertion just begun?
See, summer lies upon the land.
Why do you wheel on every hand?

O birds unheeding in the skies
What takes you on your long journeys?

Your knowledge takes our carefreeness,
For if you know, how can we less
Take thought for winter's bitterness,
Or go on trusting sun's caress?

O birds already in the skies
What sends you on your long journeys?

Take sun and leaves and light away
And gradually through the turning day
The slowing sphere will silent lie
Beneath a cold malignant eye.

O birds departing through the skies
What do you take with you on your long journeys?

Weather talk

Parent: 'The cold comes from the ice, you know
The wind brings it along
This air is blowing off the snow
Packed round the drear North Pole.'

Child: 'How long does the wind take to come
From all those miles away?
The gale that's rushing down our street,
Where was it yesterday?'

Parent: 'Oh that depends on what it finds
To lash at or to goad,
And whether it meets other winds
To fight along the road.

If I could turn the skies around
I'd make this wind go back
To the blank ice that sent it here
Along its dark cold track

And get a soft breeze from the South
To come up here instead
And bring the summertime and flowers
And warm your pretty head.'

The storm

Grey shadows bold stalked over the mountain
From the twilight;
Giant shadows widely spread strode on the land,
Bringing the night.

Rain driving furious lashed at the rattling doors,
Entering unbidden;
High in the stormy night Nature made war
And all light was hidden.

Tall stately trees crashed deep in the forest,
The savage wind's prey;
Small furry animals scurried and hid,
Fear-frozen they lay.

. . . .

Strong serene sunlight filled all the heavens,
Joyfully bright;
Light filtered through the trees dappling the leaves,
– Fled was the night.

Chorale

Oh what a syllabub
Hubbub
Bubbling and quetching of birds;
Of water gurgling
In gutters and chatter
And clatter of children
At break-time over the wall;
And no doubt patter
Of insect legs drumming
Against twigs, in ricks
Of tickling straw
In this great appetite, this
Greedy maw
Called spring,
Calling for more, for everything
To be up and doing
Like me like me like me
The blue tit insists;
And in the evening
Before the dark comes down
Again with a bit
Of winter again
The blackbirds call
I am all yours
All yours, you-all.

Seasons

Skip, skip, the dairy skip
Hum, hum, the aeroplane
Munch, munch cows in long grass
Hot red light tumbling over
Insects and grass, flowers and bumbling clover,
Smell:
    summer has come again.

Crack, crack winter wind
Huddle, huddle sheep in pen
Moan, moan draughty door
Dark and groping winter forms
Wrapped around in inside rooms
Musing:
    the bright year won't come again.

Spitter, spatter click and clatter
Birds in hedges and in gutter
Seeds popping, nice rain plopping
Husks falling, leaves stretching
Children wheeling in the rain
Roads streaming, puddles gleaming
Doors slamming, voices calling
Flowers and legs visible, eyes shining
In open faces:
    fresh new year again.

Break in drought

Yellow china chimney pots
Gleam against a purple sky;
Below the trees grow greener.

Coloured like a picture book
A double rainbow cuts the sky.
In the dusty gutters winks
The rain that lifts the poppy head.

Miles from gardens green or brown
Seamen listen to the wind.
Rain in summer welcomes home
Ghosts who ceased to visit here.
Rain in summer breaks the drought
And lifts the powerful poppy head.

Far beyond these present thoughts
And the blackbird's jubilation
A small child stands to watch the rain
And make a place for ghosts to come.

Towards the end of summer

Cherry red and honey bee
Buzzed around the summer flowers
Bumbled round the luscious fruits.
Patient weaver clambered by.

Silently while the others bobbed
And busied in the bright blue air
Hither, zither, merrily,
Weaver waved his cool brown arms
And gently drew around the tree
Silken skeins so fine so fine
No one could see that they were there,
Until one autumn morning when
Cherry was gone and bee asleep
A silver shawl was laced across the grass
With little beads like pearls strung all along.

Going out with Mum

'Still got the umbrella Dad gave me last Christmas.
Just fetch my gloves dear, no, the leather ones,
The ones I went to Baker Street to collect
And the man said "All change" and wouldn't let me stop
To think if I had everything.
Look in the other drawer. Have you seen my purse, John?
I know I had it. I'd just paid the milkman
And the phone rang. Look in the bathroom then.
Keys, money, letters. Have you got handkerchiefs?
Don't sniff, Bridget, blow. I must make sure
I've got the address right. D'you think you'd better take macs?
Just put the bread knife away dear, you never know
Who may get in and if they see one handy
It might – no, leave the kitchen window
There's the cat.'

We round the corner as the bus pulls off
From the bus stop. 'Now if you'd been ready
We might have caught that. It would have made all the
   difference.
There might not be another one for hours.'

We almost believe it's true it was our fault:
Mum's too good at being efficient for it to be hers.

It's the cupboard

There's a small tin of salt or such
That my Mum uses all the while
It always gets behind things that are much
Bigger, like cereal packets, or the pile
Of old odd saucers that she never uses.

Perhaps it's the way the cupboard is made
That the little things like to hide behind
A large tin of extra marmalade
That's been there for a year, not the kind
We like, yet she can never find her glasses.

My Mum is keen on law and order
And has a place for everything
In kitchen drawer and desk and larder
For her key and pen, for her purse bag and ring.
So the reason for so much going astray
Must be
Because the cupboard's made that way.

Can you count?

I went into the kitchen where my Mum had been cooking
And I counted five cakes:
One for my Dad when he comes in from work,
One for Ann when she comes home from school
One for her friend who comes with her, usually,
And one for me.

So I got up on a chair and I counted again:
Five cakes on a plate
Set out so nicely, and my Mum had put icing
And each had a cherry.
One two three four (Dad, Ann, her friend and me).
There was an extra one, one for one more
So I couldn't resist and I ate it.

I went into the kitchen where my Mum had been cooking
Five pots of jam:
One for Granny when she comes to stay,
One for next door's in return for some fruit,
One for the hospital when my Mum visits there,
One for the cupboard to keep till Christmas.
I thought I would put the fifth on the shelf
To help my Mum, but I dropped it.

Dad came in from work
Mum came home with Ann
And Ann had brought her friend.
One two three four people coming in to tea
And me.
Mum looked at the plate.
Mum looked at the floor.
We were very sad. I bent down my head.
'Five people, four cakes, one smashed jar of jam
When you counted you forgot me,' Mum said.

Arithmetic lesson – old sort

A penny and a penny makes two pennies.
Twopence was a phone call.
Two pennies plus two pennies make four pennies
Fourpence was a lolly.
Fourpence and fourpence is eightpence
Eightpence would get you there and bring you back.
Eight pennies and eight pennies make sixteen
Sixteen pence was dinner at school + 1.

And if you went on like that, carefully
Adding a penny to a penny
(And carefully checking that your addition was right)
You got to £1 + £1.
For £2 you used to get
A week at the seaside or something like that, but now
(And that, mind you, was even before I was born)
Now £2 would give you a short time at the fair
Or half a pair of second-hand jeans, or a dog.

Well, say you had persisted and been lucky
And got to £1,000 and £1,000; and then some more
You could buy a house and when you had saved up for paint
Start painting your own front door.
So a penny and a penny is a house.

I think it's worth it, don't you? But you have to remember
That getting as far as that means
You can't stop on the way and have a phone call
A lolly, bus rides, dinner, holidays, roundabouts, dogs
Or even
Half a pair of jeans.

When you are all away my dears

When you are all away my dears
I'll go from room to room
Sort out the marbles from the socks
Unposted letters from the books
Gloves from the bottom of the bed
With many lost things buried,
(And my fur hat on old fur Ted)
Fifty soft animals, some with ears
Some leaking, some with balding pelts
And pinafores tied round with belts
And knotted string round table legs
Like some worn lace gone wrong.

When you are all away, my dears
The things will stay in place
And oh, how nice to do things once
Go out, and find when I come in
A room has the same face.
I'll straighten all, then live like a queen
Surveying my domain.
I'll breathe, admire; and then I'll wait
For you to come again.

All the gear

I saw a lovely pair of boots
Round a lovely pair of legs
Out of the boots came the nicest breeches
Close but not too tight
Just so, just right
Then a neat little back
And on the back lying in a straight line
Just-so fair hair, combed and fine.
'Oh if I had those legs and those shoulders
Those good boots and fitting jacket
I would walk and walk and walk straight ahead'
I said.
The head turned, the hair swept aside like a curtain
Showing the face
'My feet and my thoughts are tired tired tired' it said.

Legs like a friend of mine

In front of me on the pavement suddenly your legs
(Long ago friend)
Legs with no ankles, plonking firmly on
(I push through the crowd)
One set of toes turned in a little bit
(I call your name out so as not to miss you).

I get round to the other side and too late to halt my greeting
An ugly face looks crossly into mine.

My friend from long ago, you would long ago have told me
It is not considered a reason among grown-ups,
To say, when one embraces a stranger,
'You've got legs like a friend of mine.'

Changes

My butterfly brooch is flitting off
Through the open window;
The hedgehog from the hearthstone moved
Sure though slow;
The bird in the picture on the tree
Has gone, and the real sea
Must have taken back the crabs and shells
We put in the pebble-filled watery jars.

Where, you ask, have our creatures gone?
They moved away when you left home.

The uninvited

What are all these uninvited guests doing
Swarming through my life, up my stairs
Telling me how badly I have done things
Using my stores, pushing away my furniture and carrying
Boxes they shoulder into the middle of my rooms, unpacking
Immovable objects so I cannot get through doors.
Here they stand at every corner with lists of things to blame
    me with
Appearing in the street and stopping me from getting to
    work where others
Blame me for that. I weep in corners, oppressed.

The early morning is cold and wet and depressing.
I hardly dare move my timorous limbs for dread
I will bring some fresh disdain.
I listen to the rain
And as each real minute seeps in with it someone says:
'They have all gone. The day is yours again.'
I look round and it is so, and the voice is mine.
I wake, glad to be so, glad even of rain and cold
And work and dirt and gloom.
I am ready to praise anything, for oh Heaven,
That terrible gang has gone.

The hunter evades the guardians

Pit pat tabby cat
Tip top pitapat
Tiptoed through the grass
Up and over
The wall
That straight and tall
And spiked with glass
Held the garden.

Hidden in a green-house
Closed in by darkness
Man and long-haired pussy-cat
Ill-intentioned, waiting:
A snarl
Oh well-kept puss, a gnarl
On an old hand that
Clutched a truncheon.

'Pst here he comes now
Just watch and see how
He takes my birds, my mice.
Digging up my seedlings!
Vandal –
What a scandal!
Deep-dyed vice
Must be dealt with.'

Proud lithe animal
Silkily along the wall
Untouched by glinting glass
Noticed his enemies.
He leapt
A shadow crept
Behind tall grass
Into the garden.

Seven nonsense animals

Cat

Old mat
Sandy cat
Hissed and spat
And that was that.

Snake

Slithery slithy
Along the highway
Much too myvy
Always in ivy
Not quite arrivy.

Dog

In a bog
Woofly dog
Afraid of the frog
Slept like a log.

Pigeon

Dirty tove
Fussing strove
Valiant to prove
And rascal in love
But didn't move.

Old Pig

Not put out
Smiling and stout
Sparring to sprout
Turned round about
And put the light out.

Fox

Nimble and cool
Nothing a fool
None, or the whole
Perceptive and cruel
Dyed out of the wool.

Man

But tyrannous fare
Are the fits from afar
That we never see near:
The blue girdy-star
That will never appear
Whose creatures we are.

Mechanics

Going, going up
Oh *what* a super lift.
Right to the top,
Right in one go
Without stopping, though
We don't want to go
Right through the roof into the cold air.
The relief of getting
Out of that dark furniture basement with square
Heavy armchairs herding you to the centre! Oh
It's dropping.
Where's the rope?
No hope of stopping
This box without handles
From crashing.
(You could at least sit in those dark brown chairs).
Screw your eyes up
Press hands on ears
Sink head in neck
For the fearful crunch
O

   o

    o

     o o o

        o   h!

       o

      o

Swaying a little
Slightly sick but still on feet that seem still to be feet
Still, it seems, in one piece and carrying parcels
Here we come out on one of the middle floors
Ready for lunch.

Recipes

To make a cake
Take
½ lb flour

To make a summer pudding
Put
In a basin
Some bread and soak

To make a summer
Take
Half an hour
Soak
In the sun that is squeezing through a gap in the houses

Shut your eyes
And your summer is ready.

Sun and rain: yes and no

Standing on the platform
Waiting for the train
I look into the puddles
Made by the rain –

Made by the rain falling
Into the dips in the ground.

I see a bit of blue sky
Beyond a castle wall
And a shimmer and sheen of green leaves
Waving over all

Then rain splashes break my picture
Falling without a sound,
The rain says no to that castle
But the sun says yes.

I look back from my puddle
And see the station wall
With groundsel and other weeds
Straggly and tall

A concrete pillar was my castle rock
A green poster my trees.

The country in the puddle
Is changing again
A great foot has stepped in it
And here is the train.

The speed makes up the picture
Of any station that I know
And the sun shines shouting 'Yes'
Though the rain says 'No'.

Looking at pictures

I would like a walled garden with flowers hanging
In cascades down white-washed pillars in the sun.
I would like hounds on leashes.
I would like not to be me.

But if I lived in a past age and had another body
Perhaps I would look *out* of this picture book and think
'I would like a world where babies did not die, where
Children were not whipped and where people believed what
    was true.
I would like not to be "important" and afraid; to play in the
    street
And laugh without hiding bad teeth and have clean hair
And go in for my tea when someone called, instead of
    ordering it.
Oh beautiful tough and lucky little children
I would like to be *you.*'

In a dark stone

'About seven thousand years ago
There was a little girl
Who looked in a mirror
And thought herself pretty.'

'I don't believe you. All that time ago
If there was a little girl she'd be wild
Wearing skins, and living in damp woods.'

'But seven thousand years ago
When England was a swamp with no one in it,
Long before the Romans,
In other lands by rivers and in plains
People made necklaces and learnt to write
And wrote down their accounts, and made fine pots,
Maps of the stars to sail by, and built cities;
And that is where they found this mirror
Where once the Hittite people roamed and ruled.'

'So you were there, were you, all that time ago
And living far from home, in ancient Turkey?'

'No, but I saw this mirror. Here in England.
It was the smallest thing in a large hall
Of great bronze cauldrons, statues, slabs of stone.
You mustn't think that it was made of glass
Common, like our mirrors.   It was
A little lump of stone, shining; black; deep;
Hard like a thick black diamond, but better: obsidian.
It would have fitted in the palm of your hand.
One side was shaped and polished, the back rough.

Small though it was I crossed the room to see it.
I wanted to look in it, to see if it worked
Really, as a mirror, but I waited.'

'Why did you wait till nobody was round you?
You weren't trying to steal it were you?'
                                    'No. I was scared.

I waited and came slowly to it sideways.
I put my hand in front. It worked as a mirror.

And then I looked into that polished stone.
I thought the shadow of the shape I looked at
Was looking out at me. My face went into
That dark deep stone and joined the other face
The pretty one that used to search her mirror
When she was alive thousands of years ago.

I don't think she'd have come if there'd been a crowd.
They were all looking at the gold and brass.'

'I wish I could see it. Would she come for me?'

'I think the mirror's back in Turkey now.'

'I'd travel miles and miles if I could see it.'

'Well, nearer home, there were flint mines in Norfolk
And just where the land slopes a bit above some trees
On the Suffolk–Norfolk border, there's a track
And once I saw . . . But that's another story.'

Mr Chatty

We knew a man called Mr Chatty
Which was funny because he didn't
Say much.
We used to wonder why he was called that. He
Sometimes gave us pennies and said
'Off you go now!' but I never thought
My sister would say out loud in front of him
'Why are you called Chatty when you don't?'
He smiled at me. 'Well, if I was called Mr Bad
Would you want me to be bad?' he said
To her. I wished I could have caught
My sister out with clever words like that.
'Mr Chatty didn't use to chat,'
I told her the other day, 'because he thought.'

Warning

When I am an old woman I shall wear purple
With a red hat which doesn't go, and doesn't suit me.
And I shall spend my pension on brandy and summer gloves
And satin sandals, and say we've no money for butter.
I shall sit down on the pavement when I'm tired
And gobble up samples in shops and press alarm bells
And run my stick along the public railings
And make up for the sobriety of my youth.
I shall go out in my slippers in the rain
And pick the flowers in other people's gardens
And learn to spit.

You can wear terrible shirts and grow more fat
And eat three pounds of sausages at a go
Or only bread and pickle for a week
And hoard pens and pencils and beermats and things in boxes.

But now we must have clothes that keep us dry
And pay our rent and not swear in the street
And set a good example for the children.
We must have friends to dinner and read the papers.

But maybe I ought to practise a little now?
So people who know me are not too shocked and surprised
When suddenly I am old, and start to wear purple.

Tramp

It would be pretty to have roses
Flourishing by my back door.
It would be nice to have a well-kept house
With velvet chairs not scraping a polished floor.
It would be lovely to sit down at dinner
Grey tie, pearl pin, fresh shirt and well-kept hands
And good to have a purring car in a clean garage
Eye-catching as the best brass bands.

But to keep it all going would be a lot of worry
And anyone who does it has to race and scurry
Seeing to roofs and pruning, maintenance and mechanics,
A shower of rain, a little greenfly bring on terrible panics
And ruin and failure shadow every path.

So I think this is the best thing to do:
As I walk down roads I see so many flowers
Nod-nodding in all the gardens that I pass.
I can glance into other people's rooms that they have
    furnished
And look how courteously that man is turning
To open the front door to his gleaming house.
Did you see how his suit fitted him, his perfect cuffs?
    Spotless cars
Slide by with women in furs and perfumes
Wafted to me with the flavour of cigars.

I am wrapped in my layers of shapeless coats
And I need never polish or dig or set
The table out for four distinguished guests
Or get to an office or prove myself each day
To provide for hammocks and lawns,
To get my antiques protected against insects.
A guest everywhere, I look in as dinner is served.
As I tramp past others' gardens, the rose opens.

Old man by the fire

Sitting, I was, by my fire
Thinking I'd maybe make another pot
To go with a taste of one of them nice little biscuits
Madge got a tin of for the grandchildren's Christmas;

Thinking that once you decide you're not going out
You can get to prefer to stay in. I'd said no to Madge
Almost from habit, 'no', I said, 'I'll not go.'
It's different in summer, besides I could get something done.
'I won't know anyone, and there's the problem of clothes.'

And strange – perhaps the gas fire and too much tea –
But I heard a voice I hadn't thought of for years.
'Oh come on,' it said, 'you are an old stick-in-the-mud.
Of course you've got something to wear – why, someone
    with style
Could wear those silk pyjamas and look good,
A hat at a different angle, a scarf tied sideways
A blanket for a scotch plaid – they'll think it's a fashion,
Anyway, I'd like to go, and you can't make a party
If everyone stays at home.' I let her dance on,
Kind and courageous, dance on out of my life,
Worrying about myself, not caring for her.
I hope she had a good life – I heard later
The world was not always particularly kind to her.

'Madge, is that you? There's tea in the pot if you want.
Eh, Madge, do you remember whether I kept that suit,
The white linen one I bought when we went to Spain?
I *know* it's winter, Madge, I'm not that daft.
I pay the gas bill don't I? To wear, of course,
I just fancy dressing up for that Christmas party.
What does it matter if I do feel tired the next day?'

November returns

Firework time, and this year, gales.
Large trees dip and bow tearing their leaves
Against the air, which seems to thicken now.
Not a quiet time even when the weather is quiet.
Fireworks, and your birthday: the year beginning
Apart from the calendar. A time when things have happened.
Advenire, Advent: to come to reach to happen.

Some years there is sunshine pale in woods.
It lies in splashes like paint on leaves, on the track,
A pausing in the year before it swings
Down to the dark,
And the leaves thin – beech-gold, pebble-brown
A clearing in the grove.
On some dim soft dun afternoon
Having to wait for something, you go for a stroll
At the back of the Works ('back in twenty minutes').
An astounding tree picked out by secret sunshine
Makes sense of the Golden Bough, the magic in woods.

Bonfires, Hallowe'en past, children running through streets,
Something stirring in the blood that makes us rise
And stand at the window, leaving the curtain ajar,
Expectant of something, watching, waiting
For something to happen; someone, perhaps, to arrive.
Maybe it is just the wind shifting direction
Dropping leaves at doors, pattering rain on the windows.

I draw the curtains, light the fire, for you
And others I have lit for at this time:
Ghosts returning to their winter quarters
To keep me company, to celebrate the season.

Poem for an old enemy

Although I did not like you, Monkey Puzzle,
Thinking a tree to be a lush and shady thing
In the green England I grew up in,
Finding your iron spikes not right, too bold
On the lawn of my childhood,
Dusty Monkey Puzzle Tree
I regret your passing.

Seeing you in this other garden I go past now
Every day to work, I am reminded –
I am reminded of the surprise
Of thinking of trees and plants that were not green,
Without a smell or soft moist earth round roots;
Of a tree, not-a-tree, that must always have been old.

Now here I look as usual from the bus
One morning, and don't believe – but you are gone.
And why should I be sorry, who never liked you
Personally, Monkey Puzzle Tree?

Because I remember the hours I spent looking
At your crazy branches; trying to find the way
If I had been a monkey, that I would have gone.
And so your dingy and depressing arms
Still make me think of the courage of persistent people who pit
Human wit
Against impenetrability.

Hare and Tortoise

Stay close, little tortoise, dig in,
Put on the coffee pot fourteen times a day
Day and night intermingled with much slow pottering.
Put your nose out rarely

So that in the spring
There will be someone calm to note the spot
Where my beautiful friend the hare
Died galloping across the frozen hills.
Stay close, little tortoise, stay alive,
Collect your strength, drip, drip, through months, in a phial
To sing a dirge for our beautiful friend the hare.

Another story of Hare and Tortoise

There was something I forgot to tell you when I told you the
    story
Of the hare and tortoise. You remember,
How the one animal, splendid, desirable, eager
Life tingling in its limbs, was admired by all
And how the other
Arrived when nobody was actually looking.

They said it was his desire to win – obstinacy.
Nobody else was there. He said he got there.
We were all gathered round the starry hare
Succouring his weakness.
(His faint was only a lapse; he was a splendid runner.)
But even if it's true what tortoise said
We were not there to greet him at his win.
The world had gone elsewhere
We wanted to be with hare.

The loneliness of saying 'I won' to nothing but emptiness!
He wasn't liked. He worked for what he got
And always so damned fair.
It was much more fun with hare.

Story

Off she goes, my little Red Riding-Hood
Cased in jeans, cheeky, with smiles and joy
To see her Gran.
Oh, wolf, be friendly.
She thinks she is tough enough
To eat you up – irresistibility
(How can she not be? She thinks she's the cat's whiskers)
Itself.
Couldn't you, just for once, stay away wolf?

Another story of Red Riding-Hood

I know a girl who's fit to eat
I know a girl with good strong feet
For walking;
I know a girl with sparkly eyes
I know a girl who doesn't tell lies,
My darling.

I know a wolf in a forest lair
Plotting and planning with great care
For dinner
To trick a girl who's thoughtful and kind.
It's always in her Grandma's mind
To win her

Away from the dangers of the wood
And keep her safe if only she could
Protect her.
The wolf is slinking through the trees
And he must hurry if he's
To collect her.

The girl, too sensible to stay
And dilly-dally on the way,
Was singing.
Her bag held her and Granny's luncheon
From it her father's hawthorn truncheon
Was swinging.

This was the song that she sang to the wolf
To the hungry wolf who grumbled and snarled:

You are bad and I am good
You stay in your part of the wood,
I'll keep my way.
You can have my sandwiches for lunch
(They're juicier than Gran's bones to munch).
Then go away.

She shouted and waved her stick and danced
And the wolf saw a pigeon, as it chanced,
Deep in the wood.
Thinking as always about her Gran
Like a mile-a-minute sprinter ran
Red Riding-Hood.

A spell

From the horrors of the night
Daylight wake you.
From paralysis of fear
Action shake you.

From the cruelty within
May love protect you.
Of the uncharity of sin
Let none suspect you.

Against the feverish clutch of greed
Pray kindness ward you,
And your care for those in need
Help to safeguard you.

Through the turbulence of desire
Steadfastness hold you
And from the slimy cling of mire
Some health enfold you.

May you not be too much harmed,
Whatever's sent you,
To breathe and flourish, and have charmed
Days that content you.

Queen of Hades, Persephone's song

Every step I take
Somewhere hedges break
Out into myriad leaves;
The soil heaves
With every step I take.

Every breath I draw
Somewhere glaciers thaw
Into a thousand streams;
Sleep is shot with dreams
At every breath I draw.

Every leaf I make
Every babe I wake
I push from dust;
Back to my store must
Come every leaf I make.

Invitation to a birthday party

Come and wet a baby's head
    Just born
    Keep her warm
Wish she may be fairly led
    To do no harm.

Drink to wet a baby's head
    Wise and still
    Hold her close
Wish her luck and share the bread
    Of good will.

Wish her luck and wish her care
To use such luck as she may get.
Wish her safety, but with dare
Enough to make the laughter set
Glasses tinkling, spires upshooting
Birds a-shouting, sunrise sparkling
Money jingling, people dancing
Early rise and late to bed.

Fools and rogues lie thick in store
There's a new one twice a minute
Why should families want more?
You'd have thought they'd reached the limit.
But each baby needs a chance
For celebration: song and dance,
So with the party spirits pour
Blessings on *this* baby's head.

Lullaby

Baby, hush now; sleep for your sister, sleep now,
Baby, dear one, peacefully on my arm.
Baby, hush now; sleep for your brother, sleep now,
Baby, darling, we'll keep you safe from harm.

Baby, hush now; listen to what I'm saying
When you're bigger I hope we'll always be friends.
When you're bigger come with us when we're playing
Baby, hush now; sleep till the darkness ends.

Baby, hush now; sleep for your sister, sleep now,
Baby, dear one, peacefully on my arm.
Baby, hush now; sleep for your brother, sleep now,
Baby, darling, we'll keep you safe from harm.

Sleep, now

Hush-a-bye hush-a-bye
Never mind the noise
Hush-a-bye hush-a-bye
Never mind the cries.

Cuddle up cuddle up
Mummy's here to stay
Rock-a-bye, rock-a-bye
Send you on your way.

Close your fluttery eyelids, babe,
Let them droop and stay
Closed, and we will still be here
We won't go away.

Close your eyes and sleep my love
Hush now, no more noise
Hush-a-bye hush-a-bye
Hush now, no more cries.

Rope song

Skip, skip, turn the rope
Sally's clumsy, not a hope.
Turn, turn, spin the wheel
Maisie's lazy, run and reel.

Jump a little higher, Sam
Then you'll get to where I am
Standing on a tree stump turning
Rope for you to jump, returning
In then out, wheeling, dealing

Quicker, slicker, one two three
In (turn), jump (turn), out (turn), jump (turn)
All together jump jump JUMP
Sam and Sally and Maisie.

The life of feet

Walking, walking down by the sea
Walking, walking up on the hill
Strong feet, long feet
Squat feet, young feet
Making tracks on paths
Shuffling through the leaves
Going with a purpose

Feeling the sand and the waves
Knowing the grass and the land.

Running, running in through the gate
Clattering, jumping, up to the steps
Shapely feet, firm feet
Straight feet, tired feet
Coming home after play
Up the steps to the door
Glad to have a rest

Warmed by the sand, soothed by the waves
Cooled by the grass, firmed by the land

Good strong walking feet.

A bicycle for two

('You'd look sweet
  Upon the seat
  Of a bicycle made for two'
        Daisy, Daisy)

Baby, baby, hold on tight
Whizzing down the road we go:
Stop at crossings, walk across
Up again on my steel horse
Steady, calm and slow.

Baby, baby, sit up straight
Arm out for signal, bend to the curve.
You can lean your face against my back.
Bump! Here we go on the cycle track.
Lorry, don't you swerve!

Whizzing home down the road we come
Baby, baby, hold on tight
You can put your arms around my back
And snuggle into my anorak
But baby, DON'T you bite!

Ugh!

Grubby little feet
Where have you been?
Don't you bring all that dirt in
My carpet's clean.

Sticky little hands
What's squashed up in them?
Have you taken fistfuls oozing
With butter and jam?

Dribbly chocolate mouth
(Cat that's lapped the cream)
Don't you rub your itchy face
On my arm.

Into the bath with you!
Now I can see your face.
Itch and dirt away it goes
Sand from in between your toes
Down the plughole with the water
Now there's splashing and there's laughter

And warm clean healthy feet.

Running and catching

There was a girl
And she could run as fast as anything
Faster than a racing bike.
She could leap and jump over the crags with mountain animals
But she couldn't catch a ball.

And there was a boy:
Long arms shot out, he could catch anything
Small balls on a bounce
Frisbees that whizz past your nose like speeded-up planets
But he couldn't run at all.

High in the air, low on the ground, he caught.
She leapt over fences and ran great distances.
He couldn't run for toffee, not even for a bus.
She couldn't catch, even if you gently threw her a baby's ball.

So when the time came for the summer fair, and there
        were games in the field
What should they do? They teamed up, it was obvious.
The fleet-footed, elastic-armed, catching-and-running pair
Won all the prizes, and by the next year's fair
The girl could catch balls and the boy never missed a bus.

The black-and-tan and ginger

Between the chicken coop and the fence
Draggled and perfectly regal they sat
Watching the budgerigar and hens
A black-and-tan, and a ginger cat.

His wife said she couldn't stand no more
When old Mr Rogers vanished again.
Unworried were sitting each side the back door
The ginger and the black-and-tan.

The snow went away and the spring came along.
To greet the season Lily stole a hat
And waving their tails to decide who was wrong*
Were sitting the ginger and black-and-tan cat.

The days grew warmer, the evenings light
And Annie Thomas caught her man
And nothing came to the wood that night
But the ginger and the black-and-tan.

Young Mr Brownley lost his May
And he went to his shed and there he sat
And nobody saw him night and day
But the black-and-tan and the ginger cat.

And sad or content, in love, in despair
Ordinary people along the lane
There must have been, I daresay, where
Sat the ginger and the black-and-tan.

If human frailty finally gives in
Nobody need know what I'm at
But there in the moonlight silent as sin
Sit a black-and-tan and a ginger cat.

*They said she was wrong because it was a horrible colour
and anyway, she should have stolen something useful like
fish.

If I were a witch

If I were a witch, my dear,
I'd turn you into a tree.
But being only a human
I'll plant one for you to see.

If I were a witch I suppose
I could turn myself into a beauty.
But being a middling human
All I can go on is duty.

If witches were so powerful
They would have become something good
And got on the side of the heroes
And helped them through the wood.

If they had really been powerful
They'd have turned themselves out of witches
As I would change myself into
Something better than I am.

Lady Love

O cat that's licked the cream
A dream
Of satisfaction
A gleam
In the bright eye
That sees over the hedge
Come jump-jump-jumping
Its lady love
Lady Love.

O hat that sits supreme
A-beam
On curly head
That comes up over the hedge
A bob-bob-bobbing
To see love
Lady Love.

To see her as
She rides by
Sparkles in her eye
Laughter in her face
Perfume filling all the space
Where she rides by
Lady Love's cavalcade
Where she rides by
Rides swiftly by
Moving on, going,
Love,
Lady Love
Lady Love
Lady Love.

Keep me

Keep me in wine and olives
Buy me winter hats
And you can have my brooches
My pictures and my cats

Keep me in fur and feathers
In rugs and pillows soft
And you can have my field and
The documents in my loft

Keep me in warmth and pleasure
Keep the postman coming.
When I've gone you can have the lot
If now you keep me going.

The sun has burst the sky

The sun has burst the sky
Because I love you
And the river its banks.

The sea laps the great rocks
Because I love you
And takes no heed of the moon dragging it away
And saying coldly 'Constancy is not for you'.

The blackbird fills the air
Because I love you
With spring and lawns and shadows falling on lawns.

The people walk in the street and laugh
I love you
And far down the river ships sound their hooters
Crazy with joy because I love you.

Great sun

Great sun
Eat the clouds up
So that my love can flourish with my garden,
So that my love, my love
And all the busy joy of greenery
Can flourish.

Storm wind
That brings the clouds
Huge and heavy, stifling up the heavens,
Push on, push them over
So that the flattened garden can be righted
And love recover.

Zenith – hold it

Cuckoo long gone
Summer heat upon
The land;
Harvest not yet come.

Waiting, who knows for what
To happen, at the spot
In time
We have arrived at.

If we could – Stop momentarily.
Let ourselves be
Held, moveless, in the turning hub
Of eternity.

Sing some songs

Sing some songs for children
When I've gone away.
Even this one, maybe.
Though I'm too sad to say
'Goodbye' to the children
We can sometimes sing
Lift the voice in singing
Even with heart-breaking.

Sing some songs for young girls
When I've gone away
Treat them as gold, treat them as pearls
Treat them as Queens of the May
And they will be kind and reward you
With smiles like the sun shining
And lift the voice in singing
To cheer you on your way.

Sing some songs for young men
When I've gone away
Treat them with cream, treat them with wine
And praise them as you may.
Laugh back into their laughing eyes
And they will want to sing,
Join in the strenuous singing
The songs you'll sing to the children
When I've gone away.

Jenny Joseph was born in Birmingham in 1932 but when she was two her parents moved, so she missed a city childhood. Her first remembered home was in leafy Buckinghamshire, on the edge of the Chilterns not far from the Thames. Other important childhood places were Dorset (she learnt to ride a bicycle the winter Poole Harbour froze over), and later, the North Devon coast. The school she was at was evacuated there at the beginning of the war. They could see the South Wales coast from the shore and the smoke from the fires when Cardiff was bombed.

She left school at fifteen and went abroad to learn languages, then got a scholarship to Oxford to read English. Later she trained as a newspaper reporter.

Her work was first published when she was at university in the 1950s, her first book was published in the 1960s – a decade which also included marriage, children and children's books. In the 1970s she had two volumes of poetry published and wrote *Persephone*, which later won the James Tait Black Award for Fiction when it was published in 1986.

Index of first lines

Keep me in wine and olives 74
My butterfly brooch is flitting off 32
My Dad took me to look in a shop window 8
O birds gathering in the skies 15
O cat that's licked the cream 73
Off she goes, my little Red Riding-Hood 57
Oh what a syllabub 19
Old mat 36
Pit pat tabby cat 34
Sing some songs for children 78
Sitting, I was, by my fire 50
Skip, skip, the dairy skip 20
Skip, skip, turn the rope 65
Standing on the platform 41
Stay close, little tortoise, dig in 55
Still got the umbrella Dad gave me last Christmas 23
The cold comes from the ice, you know 17
The little cats sit under the hedge 5
The sun has burst the sky 75
There was a bird and he went hop hop 7
There was a girl 69
There was something I forgot to tell you when I told you
    the story 56
There's a small tin of salt or such 24
Three wicker wands 10
To make a cake 40
Walking, walking down by the sea 66
We knew a man called Mr Chatty 46
What are all these uninvited guests doing 33
When I am an old woman I shall wear purple 47
When you are all away my dears 29
Yellow china chimney pots 21

Acknowledgements

From *The Inland Sea* (Papier Mache 1989)

Legs like a friend of mine
When you are all away
Changes
Looking at pictures

From *Selected Poems* (Bloodaxe 1992)

Chorale
Hare and Tortoise
Story
Warning
The sun has burst the sky
Tramp (original title 'Living off other people')

From *Ghosts and other company* (Bloodaxe 1995)

November returns
In a dark stone
The uninvited

Some of the poems in *All the Things I See* have appeared in:
This Poem Doesn't Rhyme ed. G. Benson; Noel Streatfield's
Birthday Book; Unzip Your Lips ed. P. Cookson; *More Words in
Edgeways* ed. B. Ricketts; *Reflecting Families* ed. J. Chernaik;
Read Me ed. G. Morgan; *Poetry Book Society Anthology* ed. J.
Barker; *Voices for Kosovo* ed. R. Loydell; *Stride; Poem for the
Day* ed. Albery; *Encounter; The Scotsman; Poetry Review; Rialto;
The Oxford Treasury of Time Poems.*

'In a dark stone' was commissioned for a children's programme by Central Television; 'Lullaby' was commissioned for *Wake up! Stir about! new songs for assembly* (Unwin Hyman); 'Chorale' has been set to music by Gregg Smith for his choir, the Gregg Smith Singers.

Let Me Touch the Sky

Selected Poems for Children by Valerie Bloom

Let Me Touch the Sky is a brand-new selection of Valerie Bloom's warm, sparky and evocative poetry which will delight readers of all ages.

Autumn Gilt

The late September sunshine
Lime green on the linden leaves
Burns bronze on the slated roof-tops,
Yellow on the farmer's last sheaves.

It flares flame-like on the fire hydrant,
Is ebony on the blackbird's wing,
Blue beryl on the face of the ocean,
Glints gold on the bride's wedding ring.

A sparkling rainbow on the stained-glass window,
It's a silver sheen on the kitchen sink,
The late September sunshine
Is a chameleon, I think.

Valerie Bloom

A selected list of poetry books available from Macmillan

The prices shown below are correct at the time of going to press. However, Macmillan Publishers reserve the right to show new retail prices on covers which may differ from those previously advertised.

Let Me Touch the Sky
Selected Poems for Children by Valerie Bloom
0 330 39216 6
£4.99

Collected Poems for Children
Gareth Owen
0 330 39230 1
£4.99

Selected Poems for Children
Charles Causley
0 330 35404 3
£5.99

A Spell of Words
Elizabeth Jennings
0 330 35422 1
£4.99

Glitter When You Jump
Edited by Fiona Waters
0 330 39991 8
£4.99

Golden Apples
Chosen by Fiona Waters
0 330 29728 7
£3.99

The Fox on the Roundabout
Poems by Gareth Owen
0 330 48468 0
£4.99

All Macmillan titles can be ordered at your local bookshop
or are available by post from:

Book Service by Post
PO Box 29, Douglas, Isle of Man IM99 1BQ

Credit cards accepted. For details:
Telephone: 01624 675137
Fax: 01624 670923
E-mail: bookshop@enterprise.net

Free postage and packing in the UK.
Overseas customers: add £1 per book (paperback)
and £3 per book (hardback)